Tastes&Flavors
of O'AHU

Tastes&Flavors
of O'AHU

MUTUAL PUBLISHING

ISBN-10: 1-56647-764-6
ISBN-13: 978-1-56647-764-2
Library of Congress Catalog Card Number: 2005937653

Photography credits:
© Douglas Peebles: pg. 1, 3, 5
From DreamsTime.com:
    front cover © cobraphoto, pg. 8 © Polina Pomortseva, pg. 10 © Leigh Anne
    Meeks, pg. 14 © cobraphoto, pg. 20 © Al1962, pg. 30 © David Smith, pg. 32 ©
    HandmadePictures, pg. 38 © Elkeflorida, pg. 44 © On Yi Chan, pg. 54 ©
    Picalotta, pg. 62 © Heath Doman, pg. 64 © Zigzagmtart, pg. 68 © Yelena
    Rodriguez, pg. 70 © Arenacreative, pg. 74 © Dušan Zidar

Design by Wanni

First Printing, February 2006
Second Printing, May 2014
Third Printing, January 2015
Fourth Printing, April 2015

Mutual Publishing, LLC
1215 Center Street, Suite 210
Honolulu, Hawai'i 96816
Ph: 808-732-1709 / Fax: 808-734-4094
E-mail: info@mutualpublishing.com
www.mutualpublishing.com

Printed in South Korea

TABLE OF CONTENTS

Desserts

Beverages & Drinks

Glossary

INTRODUCTION

Since a new generation of chefs emerged onto the local culinary scene nearly a decade ago, food has never been quite the same in Hawai'i. These progressive and experimental chefs changed the way we view, prepare, and eat local foods. They transcended traditional flavors to create contemporary ones; added an artistic touch to presentation; and took risks to make something new, something different. Most importantly, these chefs embraced the use of local fruits, produce, herbs, and seafood once not commonly used in Hawai'i's restaurants. In time, this new style of culinary art in the Islands was coined Hawaiian Regional Cuisine.

Many of these chefs learned, trained, or apprenticed right here on O'ahu, but the influences of Hawaiian Regional Cuisine extended beyond the shores of Waikīkī and now can be found in cities such as San Francisco, New York, and Tokyo. Needless to say, because of these chefs, the art of food not only flourished in Hawai'i but also changed the way the rest of the world experiences dining in a remote tropical paradise.

The discovery of art in local foods heralds the birth of culinary couture. Sauces with exotic flavors such as li hing, mango, or liliko'i dress up salads of Waimānalo greens with a unique taste. Pupu featuring local seafood—reinvented beyond poke as furikake seared 'ahi, or crab stuffed with shiitake mushrooms—accessorize main courses. Sumptuous desserts

7

of tropical fruit sorbets and chocolate, or a cup of creamy Kona coffee wraps up every meal.

From the simply hungry to the astute epicure, eating is one of the most favored and treasured pastimes for locals. Enjoying meals is the way we make new friends, celebrate special occasions, enjoy a night on the town, and take care of our families. *Tastes & Flavors of O'ahu* offers recipes for any occasion. Whether you are cooking for one, or for friends and family, expect only the best when you sit down to indulge in Hawai'i's cuisine.

TAPAS &
APPETIZERS

Poke 'Ahi
(Raw Yellowfin Tuna)
Serves 8

**A party in Hawai'i is rarely without
this Asian-flavored appetizer. Poke may be served
as a side dish as well as a pūpū.**

2 pounds fresh 'ahi, cut into 3/4-inch cubes
2 Hawaiian chili peppers, seeded and minced
1 cup minced green onion
1 tablespoon toasted sesame seeds
1-1/2 teaspoons sesame oil
3 tablespoons soy sauce

Combine all ingredients; toss to combine; chill 1 hour before serving. Adjust taste as necessary.

Tip: Fresh aku (skipjack tuna), swordfish, marlin, squid, or octopus may be substituted for 'ahi. Vegetarians may substitute tofu for 'ahi.

—*Recipe by* Muriel Miura

Lavosh

Makes about 5 sheet pans

8 cups sifted flour
3 whole eggs, beaten
1/4 cup shortening
1-1/2 teaspoons salt
3 teaspoons sugar
2 cups milk

Suggested Toppings
Sesame seeds
Poppy seeds
Nori furikake (seasoned seaweed condiment)

Combine all ingredients in large mixer bowl and mix until ingredients are well blended and forms a firm dough. Let rest 30 minutes; then roll out dough very thinly on lightly floured surface. Place on large ungreased cookie sheets and liberally sprinkle with toppings of your choice. Bake at 375°F for 15 minutes or until light golden brown.

Tip: Roll out dough on floured waxed paper for ease in transferring to baking sheet.

—*Recipe by* Muriel Miura

Kahuku Corn Smashed Potatoes

Serves 4 to 6

3 pounds potatoes, peeled and cubed into 1-inch pieces
1-1/2 teaspoons salt
3/4 cup sweet butter
1 large round 'Ewa onion, diced
2 cloves fresh garlic, peeled and minced
2 cups fresh corn kernels
1/3 cup half-and-half or heavy cream
1-1/2 teaspoons fresh cilantro, finely chopped
Salt and pepper to taste

Place potatoes in a pot with water to cover and salt. Bring to a boil; cook about 9 to 12 minutes or until fork tender.

Meanwhile, heat butter in a small skillet and sauté onions and garlic until tender, about 3 to 4 minutes. Add corn and cook for 2 additional minutes. Add cream and simmer for 1 to 2 minutes. Add cilantro; salt and pepper to taste.

Remove potatoes from heat and drain. Mash the potatoes, and add corn mixture. Serve hot.

—*Originally appeared in* Choy of Seafood

Seared 'Ahi

Serves 4 to 6

Butter Sauce
1/2 cup white wine
1 shallot, sliced
2 sprigs thyme
1 sprig tarragon
1 cup butter
Salt and pepper to taste

1 pound #1 'ahi, blocked for sashimi
2 tablespoons Cajun spice mix
Vegetable oil for frying

To prepare Butter Sauce: reduce wine with shallot and herbs until almost evaporated. Lower heat and slowly add cold butter until sauce is emulsified; season with salt and pepper. Coat 'ahi with Cajun spice mix. Heat vegetable oil in a sauté pan until smoking; add 'ahi and sear on all sides, keeping middle rare. Slice like sashimi and serve with Butter Sauce.

—*Recipe by* Chef Brooke Tadena

'Ahi Tartare with Taro Chips

Serves 6 to 8

2 pounds fresh raw 'ahi, chopped into small pieces
2 anchovy fillets, chopped
1 tablespoon Dijon mustard
1 cup chopped sweet Maui onion
3 dashes Worcestershire sauce
1/4 cup capers
1 tablespoon fresh parsley, chopped
2 tablespoons extra virgin olive oil
Salt and white pepper to taste

Combine all ingredients and gently toss to combine. Serve on taro chips.

Tip: Salmon may be substituted for 'ahi.

—*Recipe by* Jeffrey Lee

Coconut-Crusted Kahuku Shrimp

Serves 4 to 6

1-1/2 pounds shrimp, cleaned and butterflied
Salt and pepper to taste
Flour

Batter
2 cups flour
1 teaspoon salt
1 egg, beaten
1-1/3 cups water

2 cups coconut flakes spread on waxed paper or foil
Oil for deep-frying

Heat 2 inches of oil in large skillet; holding shrimp by tail, place in hot oil. Do not crowd. Reduce heat to medium and fry until golden on both sides. Drain on paper towels. Keep hot in oven until all are completed. Serve with your favorite sauce.

Recipe by Joanne Fujita

Boiled Peanuts

About 1 pound

**A great snack food for picnics and sporting events.
In kid-time days, almost everyone purchased a bag of
peanuts from the "peanut lady" who sat by the
entrance to the old stadium in Mōʻiliʻili.**

1 pound raw peanuts in shell, washed and drained
1/3 cup Hawaiian rock salt
3 star anise
1-1/2 teaspoons sugar

Place peanuts in a pot in water to cover; add salt, star anise, and sugar. Cover and bring to a boil; lower heat and simmer for 1 hour 15 minutes or until peanuts are cooked through but still a little crunchy. Drain. Refrigerate.

—*Recipe by* Muriel Miura

SOUPS & SALADS

Asparagus Soup

Makes about 1 quart

1/2 cup sliced onion
1/3 cup celery, chopped
1 clove garlic, chopped
1 bunch fresh asparagus
2 cups chicken stock
1/2 cup heavy cream
1 teaspoon thyme
1 teaspoon parsley
White peppercorns to taste
1/4 bunch fresh spinach, chopped
Salt to taste

Garnishes
Quinoa or cous cous
Small cherry or pear-shaped tomatoes
Micro or any baby greens

Lightly sweat or sauté the onion, celery, and garlic until translucent. Then chop about half of the asparagus and add to the pan. Continue to cook lightly over medium heat, but do not brown. Add chicken stock and bring to a boil. Reduce heat and simmer for 10 minutes. Next add the cream and bring to a boil. Add the thyme, parsley, and peppercorns. Continue to simmer until the asparagus is tender.

Chop the remaining half of the asparagus very small. Now add the soup in small batches to the blender. Add small amounts of asparagus and spinach while blending. Be very careful as it is best to blend while hot. After all is blended, strain the soup. Finish with seasoning, if desired.

—*Recipe by* Kāhala Mandarin

Hawaiian Bouillabaisse

Serves 1 to 2

Soup Base

2 tablespoons olive oil

1 stalk leek

1 medium round onion, chopped

2 stalks celery, diced

12 small fennel bulbs, pressed

1 cup white wine

4 ripe Roma tomatoes, peeled, seeded, and diced

1 tablespoon tomato paste

2 bay leaves

2 cloves garlic

2 medium ginger, sliced

1 quart fish stock

Salt and pepper to taste

1 pinch saffron, chopped

1 (3-ounce) piece onaga fillet

2 scallops

3 mussels

2 large Ama ebi prawns or shrimp

1 (5-ounce) Hawaiian spiny lobster tail

Garnishes
1 bunch ogo (seaweed)
3 pieces baby tubular chives

Heat the olive oil in a medium size soup pot; add the leek, onion, celery, and fennel. Deglaze with white wine. Cook until translucent. Add the tomatoes, tomato paste, bay leaves, garlic, ginger, and fish stock. Simmer for about 15 minutes; add salt and pepper to taste. Remove from heat, add saffron, strain, and set stock aside.

Bring soup to a boil over medium heat and add fish, scallops, and mussels. Simmer for a few minutes until cooked and add the shrimp and lobster. Cover and remove from heat. Place in a bowl and garnish with ogo (seaweed) and chives.

Thai Noodle Salad
Serves 8 to 10

Sauce
1/3 cup clear fish sauce (Nam Pla–Thai;
    Nuoc Mam–Vietnamese)
1/4 cup water
Juice of 5 limes
1/4 cup white vinegar
4 cloves garlic, minced
Chili sauce to taste
1/2 cup sugar

2 packages (8 ounces each) pancit rice noodles
    (Filipino rice noodles)
1 cup carrot, julienne
1 Japanese cucumber, cut into thin half-circles
1 package (12 ounces) bean sprouts
2 heads green or red leaf lettuce, torn into small pieces
1/2 cup chopped peanuts
Fresh mint and basil

Combine Sauce ingredients; mix well and set aside. Fill large
pot with water and bring to a boil. Cook noodles 10 to 15
minutes or until tender. Drain, rinse immediately with cold
water, and drain again. Combine noodles and vegetables; toss
gently. Refrigerate until ready to serve. Just before serving,
drizzle Sauce over and garnish with chopped peanuts, mint,
and basil leaves.

—*Recipe by* Muriel Miura

Spicy Mango Salad

Serves 6

1 ripe mango, peeled and sliced thinly
1 green mango, peeled and sliced thinly
1 habanero (very hot) or 2 serrano (mildly hot) chilies,
    seeded and minced
2 shallots, finely chopped
1/4 cup chopped cilantro (Chinese parsley)
1 tablespoon Thai fish sauce

Juice of 1 lime
2 teaspoons granulated sugar
Pinch of salt

Place mango slices in bowl and add remaining ingredients.
Mix thoroughly. Serve on a bed of greens.

—Recipe by Joanne Fujita

Caesar Salad

Serves 4

8 leaves Romaine lettuce, washed and torn
    into bite-size pieces
1 cup croutons

Dressing
2 cloves garlic, minced
Fresh ground black pepper and salt to taste
1 anchovy
1 teaspoon Worcestershire sauce
1 tablespoon Dijon mustard
1 tablespoon red wine vinegar
2 tablespoons extra virgin olive oil
2 tablespoons grated Parmesan cheese

In a wooden bowl, rub garlic, anchovy, salt, and black pepper to the sides of the bowl until garlic is like a paste. Add Worcestershire sauce, mustard, and red wine vinegar. While mixing, add olive oil slowly in a steady stream making sure the oil is emulsifying. Add Parmesan cheese and adjust seasoning. Add romaine lettuce and toss to coat greens.

—*Recipe by* Jeffrey Lee

ENTRÉES

Waimānalo Eggplant Pâté

Serves 6 to 8

3 pounds eggplants
3 cloves garlic, chopped
1 Maui onion, chopped
2 anchovies, chopped
2 tablespoons shoyu
1 tablespoon mayonnaise
Salt and pepper to taste
2 tablespoons extra virgin olive oil
Goat cheese (optional)
Fish sauce (Nam Pla–Thai;
    Nuoc Mam–Vietnamese), optional

Preheat oven to 350°F.

Roast 3 pounds eggplant for 25 minutes or until charred. Peel off skin.

Blend all ingredients together, except olive oil, in blender or food processor. While blending, slowly add oil like making mayonnaise. Serve as dip or on gourmet crackers or wafers.

Round Steak

Serves 4 to 6

2 tablespoons oil
7 to 9 garlic cloves, smashed
Fat from meat
4 (9-ounce) blocks round steaks
Flour
2 onions, peeled and sliced
Shoyu
Green onions, for garnish

Sauté the first three ingredients in hot iron skillet. Remove garlic and set aside in a dish.

Cut meat into blocks to fit pan. Flour meat blocks on both sides. Cook meat blocks for the same amount of time in hot skillet 4 to 5 minutes, on each side or until of desired doneness. To serve, cut meat into bite-size pieces on cutting board. Pour shoyu generously over meat (don't drown it); add onions, and garnish with green onions.

–Recipe by Uncle Larry

Grilled Steak with 'Ewa Onion Rings

Serves 4 to 6

1 cup soy sauce
1/2 cup dry sherry
1/3 cup minced fresh ginger
4 cloves garlic, minced
4 (9-ounce) T-bone steaks

In a shallow pan, combine the soy sauce, sherry, ginger, garlic, and steaks and marinate for about 2 hours.

Prepare the grill.

Onion Rings
Oil for deep-frying
4 'Ewa onions, peeled and sliced
1 cup milk
1 cup all-purpose flour
Salt and pepper

Heat the oil to 375°F in a large pan. Dip the onion slices into the milk and immediately into the flour. Shake off the excess flour and deep-fry in hot oil until crisp and golden, about 2 minutes. Drain on paper towel and season with salt and pepper while hot; keep warm.

Remove the steaks from the marinade. Grill the steaks over high heat for 3 to 5 minutes on each side or until of desired doneness. Serve with the onion rings.

—*Originally appeared in* Taste of Hawai'i

Wok Fried Salt & Pepper Kahuku Prawns

Serves 2 to 4

1 pound Kahuku prawns, antennas trimmed, shell on
Cornstarch
2 cups peanut oil
1 teaspoon ginger, chopped
1 teaspoon garlic, peeled and chopped fine
1 tablespoon green onion, chopped fine
1 teaspoon red bell pepper, diced
Salt and pepper to taste

Dredge prawns in cornstarch to coat. Set aside. Heat peanut
oil in a deep pot or wok for about 3 to 5 minutes. Sauté ginger,
garlic, green onion, and red bell pepper until lightly brown;
add prawns and season with salt and pepper to taste.
BEWARE OF THE EXPLODING ROE! Stir-fry prawns in oil
until prawns turn orange. Remove to side.

Tip: Serve with Garlic Fried Jasmine Rice (recipe on page 34).

—*Recipe by* Executive Chef Kelly Degala

Garlic Fried Jasmine Rice

Makes 2 cups

2 tablespoons peanut oil
2 tablespoons garlic, peeled and minced
2 cups cooked Jasmine rice (preferably the night before)
Salt and pepper to taste

Heat wok till lightly smoking. Add peanut oil and heat again. Add garlic and immediately begin stirring; cook for about 15 seconds, then add rice, breaking it into smaller pieces. Continue to turn over, coating with oil and garlic, for about 2 minutes. Finish with salt and pepper mix. A couple of drops of Thai chili sauce may be added, if desired. To serve, place rice in middle of plate and place prawns around.

—*Recipe by* Executive Chef Kelly Degala

50th State Braised Chicken

Serves 4 to 6

Sauce
2 cups shoyu
2 cups water
1/2 cup sherry
5 slices fresh ginger root
2 tablespoons sugar
1 whole star anise
5 green onion stalks
2 cloves garlic, chopped

1 to 3-pound fryer chicken, cleaned
Sesame oil

Combine Sauce ingredients and bring to boil. Cool and immerse whole chicken in sauce; bring to boil again. Lower heat and simmer one side for 20 minutes; turn, simmer the other side an additional 20 minutes. Turn off heat. Remove chicken from sauce. Let stand 1 to 2 hours. Brush with sesame oil. Slice and serve with sauce poured over chicken.

—*Originally appeared in* Favorite Island Cookbook 2

Chinatown Gon Lo Mein *(Fried Noodles)*

Serves 4 to 6

Most people go to Honolulu's Chinatown to enjoy a noodle dish for lunch. Gon Lo Mein is an old-time favorite.

1 tablespoon salad oil
1/2 cup chicken, slivered
1/2 cup char siu (sweet roast pork), julienne
1/4 cup bamboo shoots, sliced
1/2 cup celery, sliced diagonally
1/2 cup green onion, cut into 1-inch lengths
1/2 pound bean sprouts, washed and drained
2 tablespoons toasted sesame seeds
1 pound fresh chow mein (fried noodles)

Seasonings
1 teaspoon oyster sauce
1/4 cup chicken broth
1 teaspoon salt

Garnishes
1/4 cup Chinese parsley (cilantro)
1/4 cup char siu (sweet roast pork), sliced

Stir-fry chicken in hot oil for 2 minutes; add char siu and cook additional minutes. Add bamboo shoots, celery, green onion, bean sprouts, sesame seeds, noodles, and seasonings. Stir-fry another minute to heat through. Garnish with Chinese parsley and char siu to serve.

—*Recipe by* Muriel Miura

Bay Pasta

Serves 8

2 cups fresh basil
1/2 cup extra virgin olive oil
2 tablespoons fresh lemon juice
Salt and freshly ground pepper to taste
2 cloves garlic, crushed
2 pounds large shrimp, shelled and deveined
3/4 pound bow-tie pasta
2 cups cooked frozen peas
2 tomatoes, seeded and cut into 1/2-inch cubes

Garnishes
Fresh basil leaves
Diced tomatoes

Place basil in a food processor with 1 tablespoon olive oil and process until smooth. Remove to a bowl and add lemon juice, 1/4 cup extra virgin olive oil, salt, pepper, and garlic. Set aside. In a saucepan, sauté shrimp and garlic in remaining 3 tablespoons of oil until shrimp are opaque, about 2 to 3 minutes. In a pot of boiling salted water, cook pasta until al dente. Drain and combine with shrimp in a large bowl. Toss with basil puree, peas, and tomatoes. Adjust seasonings and garnish with fresh basil leaves and diced tomatoes.

—*Originally appeared in* Another Taste of Aloha

North Shore Barbecue Pork Ribs

Serves 4 to 6

2 whole slabs pork ribs, cut into sections of 3 ribs each
Enough water to cover ribs in stockpot
1/4 cup sea salt
2 cloves garlic, crushed
1-inch piece fresh ginger, crushed
2 stalks green onion, whole

Place ribs in stockpot with water to cover. Add salt, garlic, ginger, and green onions; bring to a boil. Reduce heat and let simmer 45 minutes to 1 hour, or until ribs are tender.

While ribs are cooking, combine all Barbecue Sauce ingredients in a saucepan; bring to a boil. Reduce heat and simmer 45 minutes to 1 hour. Strain.

When ribs are tender, remove from stockpot; cool. Brush with Barbecue Sauce and grill over hot coals on a hibachi until heated through, basting frequently while cooking.

Barbecue Sauce (Makes about 7 cups)

1 teaspoon red chili flakes
2 cans (15 ounces each) tomato sauce
2 cups brown sugar, packed
1/2 cup vinegar
1/4 cup honey
1-1/2 cups minced onion
2 teaspoons liquid smoke
2 teaspoons chili powder
1 teaspoon coarsely cracked black pepper
1 tablespoon Worcestershire sauce
1/2 teaspoon dry mustard
1 cup crushed pineapple
1 clove garlic, minced

—*Originally appeared in* Cooking from the Heart

Hawaiian Fish with Sweet-Sour Sauce

Serves 4

Sweet-Sour Sauce (see next page)
1 whole fresh fish (1 to 3 pounds)(onaga, ehu, uhu, 'ōpakapaka)
Salt and pepper to taste
3/4 cup water
2 tablespoons butter
1/2 cup diced red onions
1/4 cup diced green pepper
1/4 cup diced red pepper

Garnish
Cilantro

Heat oven to 350°F. Prepare Sweet-Sour Sauce, and set aside.
Place fish in a baking pan; season with salt and pepper. Add
water, and cover pan with foil to seal. Bake at 350°F for 25 to
30 minutes. While fish is baking, melt butter in a saucepan.
Sauté onion and peppers for 2 minutes; cook for 1 minute.
Add Sweet-Sour Sauce, and simmer for 4 to 5 minutes.
Remove fish from oven, and place on a fish platter. Pour
sauce over the baked fish. Garnish with cilantro. Serve hot.

Sweet-Sour Sauce

2 tablespoons pineapple juice

1 cup granulated sugar

2/3 cup vinegar

2 teaspoons shoyu

2/3 cup ketchup

2/3 cup water

1 teaspoon minced fresh ginger

1 clove garlic, minced

1/4 teaspoon hot pepper sauce

2 tablespoons cornstarch blended with 2 tablespoons
    water for thickening

Combine pineapple juice and sugar; bring to a boil and cook until sugar is dissolved. Add vinegar, shoyu, ketchup, water, ginger, garlic, and hot pepper sauce to mixture and bring to a boil; simmer for about 3 to 4 minutes. Mix cornstarch and water together to make paste; add to sauce and cook, stirring, until thickened. Set aside until ready to serve over cooked fish.

—*Originally appeared in* Choy of Seafood

Misoyaki Butterfish

Serves 4

Misoyaki Sauce
2 cups white miso
1 cup sake (rice wine)
1 cup sugar
2 tablespoons fresh chopped ginger
1/4 cup minced green onion

4 butterfish steaks (4 to 6 ounces each)
Vegetable oil for frying

Mix all Misoyaki Sauce ingredients together. Marinate butterfish overnight. Blot excess sauce off with napkin or paper towel. Cook fish steaks covered, in 1 to 2 tablespoons hot oil on low-medium heat for 3 minutes on each side. Serve on bed of shredded cabbage.

—*Recipe by* Chef Steven Yoshii

Chicken with Shiitake Mushrooms

Serves 4

Marinade
1 teaspoon ginger juice
1 tablespoon mirin (Japanese sweet rice wine)
1 tablespoon soy sauce
1 tablespoon cornstarch

3 pounds boneless chicken, cut into 2-inch pieces
8 to 10 dried whole shiitake mushrooms,
    softened in warm water
2 tablespoons peanut oil
1 cup sliced bamboo shoots, rinsed and sliced
Salt to taste
1 teaspoon cornstarch
1 teaspoon water

Garnish
Chinese parsley

Combine Marinade ingredients and mix well; add chicken and marinate 30 minutes. Remove mushrooms from water; reserve liquid. Remove mushroom stems and cut caps in half. Set aside. Heat 1 tablespoon oil and fry chicken until browned. Pour off excess oil and add enough water to cover. Bring to a boil, reduce heat, and simmer chicken 10 to 15 minutes. Pan-fry mushrooms in 1 tablespoon oil. Season with a little salt and a tablespoon of the mushroom liquid; cook for about 3 to 5 minutes. Add bamboo shoots and add to the chicken. Cover and cook over low heat until chicken is tender. When ready to serve, stir 1 teaspoon cornstarch into 1 teaspoon water, add, and cook until thickened. Adjust seasoning with salt and garnish with Chinese parsley.

—*Recipe by* Joanne Fujita

Maunakea Street Five Spice Fried Chicken

Serves 4

Marinade

2 teaspoons soy sauce

1 teaspoon sugar

1 teaspoon ginger juice

1 teaspoon sherry

1/8 teaspoon five spice powder

3 pounds chicken, cut in 1-1/2-inch pieces

Batter

4 eggs, slightly beaten

1 cup cornstarch

1/2 teaspoon sugar

1/4 teaspoon salt

3 tablespoons peanut oil

Mix Marinade ingredients together; add the chicken and marinate for 2 hours.

To prepare batter, gradually add cornstarch, sugar, and salt to eggs; mix well. Dip marinated chicken pieces into batter and fry in hot oil until brown and tender. Drain on paper towels.

—*Recipe by* Joanne Fujita

DESSERTS

Two-Crust Banana Pie

Serves 8

This pie is very similar to old-fashioned apple and berry pies. Once very popular, you'll hardly ever find it on restaurant menus today as most bakeries do not make them anymore.

1 recipe double crust pie pastry

Filling
3 cups firm-ripe bananas, sliced
3/4 cup pineapple juice
1/2 cup sugar
1/4 cup flour
1 teaspoon cinnamon
1/4 teaspoon nutmeg
Pinch of salt
1-1/2 tablespoons butter
1 tablespoon milk

Ice cream, optional

Preheat oven to 400°F. Prepare double-crust pie pastry as directed in recipe of your choice; set aside. Marinate bananas in pineapple juice for 30 minutes; drain. In medium bowl, combine sugar, flour, cinnamon, nutmeg, and salt; mix and toss bananas lightly in mixture. Roll half the pie pastry into 10- to 11-inch circle and place in bottom of 9-inch pie pan. Pour filling into crust; dot top with butter. Roll the remaining pie pastry into 10-inch circle and place over banana filling; flute edges to seal. Brush top with milk and cut slits to vent. Place pie pan on cookie sheet and bake at 400°F for 30 to 35 minutes or until golden brown. Serve warm or cold with scoop of ice cream, if desired.
—*Recipe by* Muriel Miura

Haupia
(Coconut Pudding)
Serves 20

A traditional Hawaiian dessert served at a lū'au.

3/4 cup fresh frozen coconut milk
1-1/4 cups water
1/2 cup plus 2 tablespoons sugar
1/2 cup plus 2 tablespoons cornstarch

Combine all ingredients in a saucepan. Cook over medium heat, stirring constantly until thickened. Lower heat and cook for 10 minutes, continuing to stir constantly to avoid lumping or burning. Pour into 8 x 8-inch dish and chill until set, about 1 hour. Cut into squares and, if desired, may be topped with crushed pineapple, peach, or mango slices to serve.

Tip: Canned coconut milk may be substituted for fresh frozen coconut milk.

—*Recipe by* Muriel Miura

Almond Tofu
(Almond Gelatin)
Serves 6

**A popular and refreshing dessert that can be found
at most Chinese restaurants in Honolulu.**

2 envelopes unflavored gelatin
3-2/3 cups water
1/3 cup sweetened condensed milk
2 teaspoons almond extract
1 can fruit cocktail, drained

In a saucepan, sprinkle gelatin over water and let stand 5
minutes; cook over medium heat until gelatin dissolves
completely, about 3 to 5 minutes. Stir in condensed milk
gradually; add almond extract; mix well. Pour into 8 x 8-inch
pan and refrigerate until firm, about 2 hours. When
congealed, cut into bite-size pieces and portion into individual
dessert glasses. Spoon fruit cocktail over to serve.

—Recipe by Muriel Miura

Coffee Jelly

Serves 4

This is an old-fashioned dessert that has recently sprung up again on the menus of some of O'ahu's eateries.

1 package unflavored gelatin
1/4 cup water
1-1/2 cups strong freshly brewed coffee
1 tablespoon Kahlua, optional
1 cup heavy cream or sweetened whipped cream
1 tablespoon Hawaiian raw sugar

Sprinkle gelatin over water; let stand 2 to 3 minutes. Pour hot coffee over softened gelatin and stir until gelatin dissolves completely. Add Kahlua, if desired. Pour into individual cups and refrigerate until firm, about 2 hours. Pour cold heavy cream over congealed gelatin to cover and top with sprinkle of 1 teaspoon sugar or top gelatin with dollop of sweetened whipped cream. Serve immediately.

—*Recipe by* Muriel Miura

Blueberry Loaf

Makes 10 to 12 slices

Grated zest and juice of one orange
1 egg, beaten, or equivalent in egg substitute
2 tablespoons salad oil
2 cups all-purpose flour
1 cup sugar
1-1/2 teaspoons baking powder
1/2 teaspoon baking soda
1/4 teaspoon salt (optional)
1/2 cup fresh blueberries
1/4 cup chopped nuts
Salt and pepper to taste

Heat oven to 350°F. Grease and flour two small loaf pans and set aside. Add enough water to orange juice to measure 1/2 cup; add egg and mix. In a separate bowl combine other ingredients until thoroughly mixed. Add orange juice and egg mixture; stir to moisten. Pour into loaf pans and bake at 350°F for 40 to 50 minutes or until wooden toothpick inserted in center comes out clean. Remove from pan and cool on rack.

Tip: May substitute cranberries for blueberries.

—*Recipe by* Galyn Wong

Waikīkī Coconut Cream Pie

Serves 8

1 prepared baked pie shell

Filling
1/2 cup sugar
3 tablespoons cornstarch
Pinch of salt
3 egg yolks
1 teaspoon vanilla
2 cups milk
Sweetened whipped cream

Mix sugar, cornstarch, salt, egg yolks, and vanilla. In a saucepan, scald milk. Add sugar and egg mixture to milk and cook over medium heat until thickened, stirring constantly. Remove from heat and cool completely. Add 1/2 cup grated coconut; mix well and pour into baked pie shell. Garnish with sweetened whipped cream and sprinkle with remaining coconut. Refrigerate.

Macadamia Nut Cream Pie

Serves 8

Filling
3 egg yolks
3 cups milk
1/2 cup granulated sugar
1/3 cup cornstarch
1/16 teaspoon salt
2 tablespoons butter
1 teaspoon vanilla extract
1 cup macadamia nuts, roasted and chopped

1 (9-inch) baked pie shell

Garnishes
Sweetened whipped cream
Coarsely chopped macadamia nuts

Combine egg yolks, milk, sugar, cornstarch, salt, and butter in saucepan. Bring to a boil over medium heat, stirring constantly. Simmer for 1 minute. Remove from heat; stir in vanilla and macadamia nuts. Cool slightly then pour into pie shell. Cover with plastic wrap and chill about 1 to 2 hours. Garnish with sweetened whipped cream and macadamia nuts before serving.

Poi Doughnuts

Makes 4 dozen

4 cups mochiko (two 10-ounce packages)
1-1/4 cups sugar
1 bag (12 ounces) poi
2 cups water (more or less as necessary)
Salad oil for deep-frying
Sugar for coating

Combine mochiko, sugar, and poi in mixing bowl. Add water
gradually and blend well until mixture has the consistency of
thick pancake batter, not watery. Drop by teaspoonfuls into
hot oil. Fry until golden brown. Drain on paper towels and
roll in sugar.

—*Recipe by* Chef Sam Choy

Malasadas
Makes 125 medium size malasadas

Yeast Mixture
3 packages active dry yeast
2 tablespoons sugar
1/3 cup warm water

Dough
3 cups milk or evaporated milk
1 stick butter (8 ounces)
12 eggs, beaten
8 cups flour
2 cups sugar
1 teaspoon nutmeg

Vegetable oil for frying

Mix yeast with 2 tablespoons sugar with warm water. Let it
stand for 10 minutes. Warm milk and butter together.
Combine with beaten eggs and add to flour and sugar
mixture. Add milk mixture then the yeast and mix dough
until combined. Cover and let it rise two times. Heat oil in
deep fryer to 375°F. Use a spoon to scoop up the dough then
gently drop in to hot oil. Toss in sugar to finish malasadas. To
create another twist add cinnamon or coco powder or li hing
powder to sugar when tossing.

—*Recipe by* Felipe Robello

Warm Chocolate-Mac Nut Brownie

Serves 6 to 8

2/3 cup all-purpose flour
2/3 cup sugar
2/3 cup semisweet chocolate morsels
1/4 cup unsweetened cocoa powder
1/8 teaspoon ground cinnamon
1/4 teaspoon baking powder
1/4 teaspoon salt
2 eggs, lightly beaten
1/3 cup vegetable oil
1/2 cup chopped macadamia nuts

Garnishes
Ice cream
Sweetened whipped cream
Fresh mint

Preheat oven to 350°F. Lightly grease 8 x 8-inch pan. In a medium bowl, mix together flour, sugar, chocolate morsels, cocoa, cinnamon, baking powder, and salt until well blended. Add eggs and oil; mix until blended; scrape into prepared pan and spread evenly. Sprinkle nuts over the top and bake at 350°F for 20 to 25 minutes or until wooden pick inserted in the center comes out with little gooey pieces clinging to it. Do not overbake. Let cool 10 to 15 minutes and cut into serving pieces. If desired, top with a scoop of ice cream or a dollop of sweetened whipped cream topped with a sprig of mint to serve.

—*Recipe by* Muriel Miura

Apple Sweetbread Pudding

Serves 8 to 10

1 loaf (1-pound) Portuguese sweetbread
2 cups apples, peeled and sliced
3/4 cup butter, divided
3 tablespoons lemon juice
1/2 cup brown sugar, packed
2 tablespoons plus 1 teaspoon cinnamon, divided
1/2 cup raisins
2 cups milk, scalded
1 cup sugar
5 eggs, beaten
1-1/2 teaspoons vanilla extract

Preheat oven to 350°F. Grease 9 x 13-inch pan; set aside. Tear bread into 2-inch pieces and place in prepared pan. In medium saucepan, sauté apples in 3 tablespoons butter and lemon juice over medium heat. Add brown sugar and 2 tablespoons cinnamon; continue to cook sauce until it thickens. Remove from heat; set aside. Spread apple mixture over bread pieces; sprinkle in raisins. Combine warm milk with remaining butter and stir until butter melts; stir in sugar. Mix together eggs and vanilla in separate bowl; add eggs and remaining 1 teaspoon cinnamon to milk mixture; stir to combine well. Pour over bread; let stand 15 to 20 minutes. Bake at 350°F for 30 minutes or until wooden pick inserted in center comes out clean. Serve warm or cold. May also be topped with a dollop of sweetened whipped cream, your favorite syrup, or sauce of your choice, if desired.

—*Recipe by* Muriel Miura

Grilled Tropical Fruits

Serves 20 (1/2 cup)

1 whole fresh pineapple, peeled, cored, and diced
5 ripe bananas, peeled, sliced, and dipped in lemon juice to
    prevent discoloration
2 firm ripe mangoes, peeled and sliced
1/4 cup butter
1/2 cup brown sugar, packed
1 tablespoon grated fresh ginger
Aluminum foil

Vanilla ice cream
Butter pound or angel food cake
Toasted grated fresh coconut

Combine fruits in a disposable aluminum pan and drain off
all juices. Set aside. In a sauté pan on low heat, melt butter
until it bubbles slightly. Stir in brown sugar and cook until
mixture bubbles again. Drain fruit juices again, then pour
sugar mixture over fruits and sprinkle with ginger. Cover
tightly with foil and pack for outdoor cooking.

Place foil-wrapped pan on hot hibachi and grill until you can
smell sugar caramelizing on fruits; do not burn sugar.
Remove foil and stir so sugar mixture glazes nicely over
fruits. To serve, spoon fruits over vanilla ice cream, butter
pound cake, or angel food cake, and top with coconut.

—*Recipe by* Chef Sam Choy

BEVERAGES & DRINKS

Honolulu Punch

Serves about 20

2 cans (46 ounces each) pineapple juice
1 bottle (28 ounces) ginger ale
Dash of grenadine
1 pint pineapple sherbet
Fresh mint
Maraschino cherries

Combine pineapple juice with ginger ale; add grenadine to tint to delicate pink. Add sherbet and serve immediately in tall glasses garnished with mint sprigs and maraschino cherry.

—*Recipe by* Muriel Miura

Mānoa Punch

Serves 6

5 cups fresh guava juice
5 cups fresh passion fruit juice
5 cups pineapple juice
1 cup fresh lemon juice
4 cups sugar
1/2 teaspoon red food coloring, optional

Combine all ingredients; mix and chill well. Pour into punch bowl with lots of ice.

—*Recipe by* Muriel Miura

Frosty Island Punch

Makes 2-1/2 gallons

3 cans (46 ounces each) orange-grapefruit juice, chilled
3 cans (12 ounces each) apricot nectar, chilled
3 quarts ginger ale
3 quarts pineapple sherbet

Combine chilled juices. Add ginger ale and sherbet just before serving.

Kāhala Coffee

Serves 4 to 6

1 slice lemon peel
1 slice orange peel
4 cubes sugar
2 whole cloves
1 cinnamon stick
1/4 teaspoon vanilla
1 cup brandy
2 cups very strong coffee

Place fruit peels, spices, 3 cubes of sugar, vanilla, and brandy
in the top pan of a chafing dish and heat. Place a 1 cube of
sugar in a ladle of brandy and ignite. When the brandy is
blazing, lower the ladle slowly into the pan. Pour the coffee in
and blend. When blaze has burned out serve at once in small
demitasse cups.

Kalamansi Soda

Serves 6 to 8

1 cup sugar
1 quart cold water
1 cup fresh Kalamansi lime juice
Club soda

Dissolve sugar in 1 cup water over heat. Add to remaining water and Kalamansi lime juice. Serve over crushed ice with a splash of club soda. Garnish with a twist of Kalamansi lime.

Glossary

A

'Ahi:
The Hawaiian name for both yellowfin and bigeye tuna. Often served in the Islands as sashimi (Japanese-style raw fish).

Ama ebi:
Japanese word for very large shrimp, 16 to 20 per pound (headless).

B

Bamboo shoots:
Cone-shaped young shoots sold fresh or in cans in Asian grocery stores.

Bean sprouts:
Mung beans that have sprouted. Available fresh or canned.

C

Char siu:
Pork or beef that has been marinated in a sweet-spicy red sauce and dried. Used in small amounts to flavor noodle dishes or as a side dish.

Chives:
Related to the onion and leek, this fragrant herb has slender, vivid green, hollow stems. Chives have a mild onion flavor and are available fresh year-round.

Chow mein noodles:
Chinese noodles generally made from wheat flour and eggs; sold dried or fresh.

Cilantro:
A pungent flat-leaf herb resembling parsley; also called fresh coriander or Chinese parsley.

Coconut:
The fruit of the coconut tree featuring a hard brown outer shell and containing white meat on the inside. The liquid extracted from shredded coconut meat can be drank as milk or used in cooking.

E

Ehu:
Hawaiian name for red snapper, delicate and sumptuous; yet lesser known than 'ōpakapaka.

F

Fish sauce:
Also called nam pla in Thai
cuisine or nuoc mam in
Vientamese cuisine. Very salty
and pungent. Made from
fermented small fish and shrimp.
Available in Asian markets.

Furikake:
A spicy Japanese seaweed-based
seasoning mix.

G

Ginger:
Fresh ginger is a brown, fibrous,
knobby rhizome. It keeps for long
periods of time. To use, peel the
brown skin and slice, chop, or
purée.

Guava:
A round tropical fruit with a
yellow skin and pink inner flesh
and many seeds. Grown
commercially in Hawai'i. The
puree or juice is available as a
frozen concentrate. Guava can
also be made into jams, jellies,
and sauces.

H

Hawaiian chili:
Small, hot, red chili pepper.
Substitute Thai chilies or red
pepper flakes.

Hawaiian rock salt:
A coarse sea salt gathered in tidal
pools after a storm or high tide.
Hawaiians sometimes mix it with
a red clay to make alae salt.
Substitute kosher salt.

Hawaiian spiny lobster:
A lobster endemic to Hawai'i that
has a purple and white-striped
tail and solid black legs; a choice
delicacy that is often preferred
over Maine lobsters by many.
Unlike Maine lobsters, Hawaiian
spiny lobsters don't have massive
claws

J

Japanese cucumber:
Smaller, thinner-skinned, and
with fewer seeds than other
cucumbers. Substitute with the
youngest American cucumbers
available, peeled and seeded.

Jasmine rice:
A fragrant and delicate Asian rice. Substitute white long-grained rice.

K

Kahuku prawns:
Farm-raised, freshwater prawns that are slightly sweeter than shrimp. Jumbo shrimp may be substituted.

Kalamansi lime:
A type of lime commonly found in Southeast Asia, native to the Philippines. It is very small, round, thin-skinned, and green in color, changing to yellow as the lime ripens. The seeds are large and account for half the volume of the fruit. The flesh is very juicy and flavorful (it tastes rather different than other limes) and is only a little acidic. Often, the lime juice is used for drinks as well as flavoring for fish, other fruits, and as a substitute for lemon.

Kona coffee:
Rich coffee made from beans grown in the Kona district on the Big Island of Hawai'i.

M

Macadamia nuts:
A rich, oily nut grown mostly on the Big Island of Hawai'i. Also called "mac nuts."

Malasadas:
A hole-less doughnut of egg-rich dough, deep-fried, and rolled in sugar; introduced to Hawai'i by Portuguese immigrants.

Mango:
Gold and green tropical fruit available in many supermarkets. Available fresh June through September in Hawai'i.

Mirin:
Sweet Japanese rice wine.

Miso:
A soybean paste made by salting and fermenting soybeans and rice. Shiro miso, or white miso, is the mildest of several different types. Available shrink-wrapped, and in cans and jars, in Asian markets. Can be stored for months in a refrigerator.

Mochiko:
Japanese glutinous rice flour used in making pastries and some sauces.

N

Nori:
Sheets of dried and compressed seaweed used in making rolled sushi. Available in Asian markets.

O

Ogo:
The Japanese name for seaweed.

Onaga:
The Japanese name for red snapper. Best steamed, baked, or sautéed. Substitute monkfish or orange roughy.

'Opakapaka:
A pink snapper with a delicate flavor. Good poached, baked, or sautéed. Substitute any red snapper, sea bass, or monkfish.

Oyster sauce:
A concentrated sauce made from oyster juice and salt, used in many Chinese and other Asian dishes to impart a full, rich flavor.

P

Pancit rice noodles:
Thin, translucent, Filipino noodles or sticks made out of rice, which are available at Asian grocery stores.

Passion fruit:
Also called liliko'i in Hawaiian. The common variety found in Hawai'i is yellow with seeds and juicy pulp inside. Passion fruit juice concentrate can be found in the frozen juice section of some markets. Substitute orange juice concentrate.

Poi:
A starchy paste made by pounding taro root with water until it reaches a smooth consistency. A staple in traditional Hawaiian diet.

Poke:
A traditional Hawaiian dish made of raw fish, Hawaiian salt, seaweed, and chilies.

Portuguese sweetbread:
Introduced to Hawai'i by Portuguese immigrants, this bread is made with sugar and honey to produce a subtly sweet flavor. It is traditionally baked as a round-shaped loaf on heated stone without a loaf tray. Typically eaten with meals and not as a dessert.

S

Saffron:
A bright yellow-orange spice that is considered the world's most expensive spice. Required in tiny amounts in most recipes.

Sake:
Clear Japanese rice wine. Other strong clear liquors such as tequila or vodka can be substituted.

Sesame oil:
Oil pressed from sesame seeds is available in two forms. Pressing the raw seeds produces oil that is light in color and flavor and can be used for a wide variety of purposes. Oil pressed from toasted seeds is dark in color with a much stronger flavor.

Sesame seeds:
Small, flat, oval, white or black seeds used to flavor or garnish main dishes and desserts.

Shiitake mushroom:
The second most widely cultivated mushroom in the world, medium to large with umbrella-shaped, flopped tan to dark brown caps with edges that tend to roll under. Shiitakes have a woodsy, smoky flavor. Can be purchased fresh or dried in Asian groceries. To reconstitute the dried variety, soak in warm water for 30 minutes before using. Stem both fresh and dried shiitakes.

Soy sauce:
A dark salty liquid made from soybeans, flour, salt, and water. Dark soy sauce is stronger than light soy sauce. A staple in most Asian cuisines. Also called shoyu.

Star anise:
Brownish seeds with eight points that taste like licorice.

....

T

Taro:
A starchy root of the taro, called kalo, is pounded to make poi. Its flavor is similar to artichokes or chestnuts. The leaves (lū'au) and stems (hāhā) are also used in cooking. Taro contains an irritating substance and must be cooked before any part of the plant can be eaten.

Taro chips:
Fried thin slices of taro.

Tofu:
The Japanese name for soybean curd. Available fresh in Asian markets.

....

U

Uhu:
Hawaiian name for parrotfish, usually served steamed, Chinese-style.